W0081410

PRAISE FOR *SHADE IS A PLACE*

"Tolbert's quietly moving collection brings us 'leaf by leaf' into a local history whose most telling and compelling archive is rooted in the ground. The poems record her relationships with the oaks, willows, and redbuds planted in Charlottesville's Downtown Mall, and with the community of people who join her for the 'shade walks' she takes to deepen her understanding of what these trees give and need. Writing in the traditions of both Black Nature and Black Feminist Thought, Tolbert uses simple yet powerful language to open our eyes to the life cycle of trees in her small Southern city's ecology, inviting us repeatedly to 'look up.'"

—Evie Shockley, author of *suddenly we*

"Every book, in a sense, is made from trees. But *Shade is a place* is also made by and for trees, wrought from studious attention to their life-giving powers, communal intelligence, and symbolic histories. In her startlingly original debut, Tolbert draws on her experience leading community 'shade walks' through the Charlottesville Tree Commission in her native Virginia, studying and extolling these sources of shelter and breath. *Shade is a place* consciously extends the American tradition of documentary poetics, plaited here with a Black feminist, ecopoetic vision distinctly Tolbert's own. 'Tell the trees I'm sorry / for taking so long to see them,' she writes, casting us in the brilliant shade of her devotion to the world, and illumining even its darkest reaches with loving regard. This is simply an extraordinary book."

—Maggie Millner, author of *Couplets*

"MaKshya Tolbert's *Shade is a place* feels like a surreal commentary on clearings. First, a clearing in the Toni Morrison sense, a necessary gathering site of deep renewal. Also, a reflection on clear-cuttings of trees, entire forests, neighborhoods, what is left behind in the absence of shade. And what becomes possible. As the lyric says, 'I saw the tree into a book / read its log / simple language' breathing, opening 'diffuse-porous' creating soft tension, layers. Sprawling throughout these lovely poems and prose, there is a pulsating ecosystem, a careful reforestation. Or, slow serene beauty, like the delicate bark of a rainbow eucalyptus."

—fahima ife, author of *Septet for the Luminous Ones*

PENGUIN BOOKS

SHADE IS A PLACE

MaKshya Tolbert practices poetry and placemaking in Virginia, where her grandmother raised her. She is the 2025 Art in Library Spaces Artist-in-Residence at the University of Virginia, and co-stewards Fernland Studios, an open-ended studio insistent on rest, rejuvenation, and reciprocity as a core compositional practice. Tolbert was the 2024 New City Arts Fellowship Guest Curator, and served as 2024–25 chair of the Charlottesville Tree Commission. She has received fellowship and residency support from the U.S.-Italy Fulbright Commission, New City Arts, Community of Writers, and Nelson Byrd Woltz Landscape Architects. Her recent poetry and prose can be found at *Poem-a-Day*, *Emergence Magazine*, *West Branch*, *Poets for Science*, and *Ran Off With the Star Bassoon*. She holds degrees from Stanford University, the University of Virginia, and the University of Gastronomic Sciences. *Shade is a place* is her first book. In her free time, she is elsewhere—a place Eddie S. Glaude Jr. calls "that physical or metaphorical place that affords the space to breathe."

The National Poetry Series was established in 1978 to ensure the publication of five collections of poetry annually through five participating publishers. The Series is funded annually by the Academy of American Poets / Amazon Literary Partnership, William Geoffrey Beattie, the Gettinger Family Foundation, Bruce Gibney, the Stephen and Tabitha King Foundation, Anna and Olafur Olafsson, Penguin Random House, the Poetry Foundation, the Gil Schwartz Foundation, and the National Poetry Series Board of Directors.

THE NATIONAL POETRY SERIES
WINNERS OF 2024 OPEN COMPETITION

Shade is a place by MaKshya Tolbert
Chosen by Maggie Millner for Penguin Books

Games for Children by Keith S. Wilson
Chosen by Rosalie Moffett for Milkweed Editions

82nd Division by D. M. Aderibigbe
Chosen by Colin Channer for Akashic Books

Blue Loop by AJ White
Chosen by Chelsea Dingman for University of Georgia Press

Our Hands Hold Violence by Kieron Walquist
Chosen by Brenda Hillman for Beacon Press

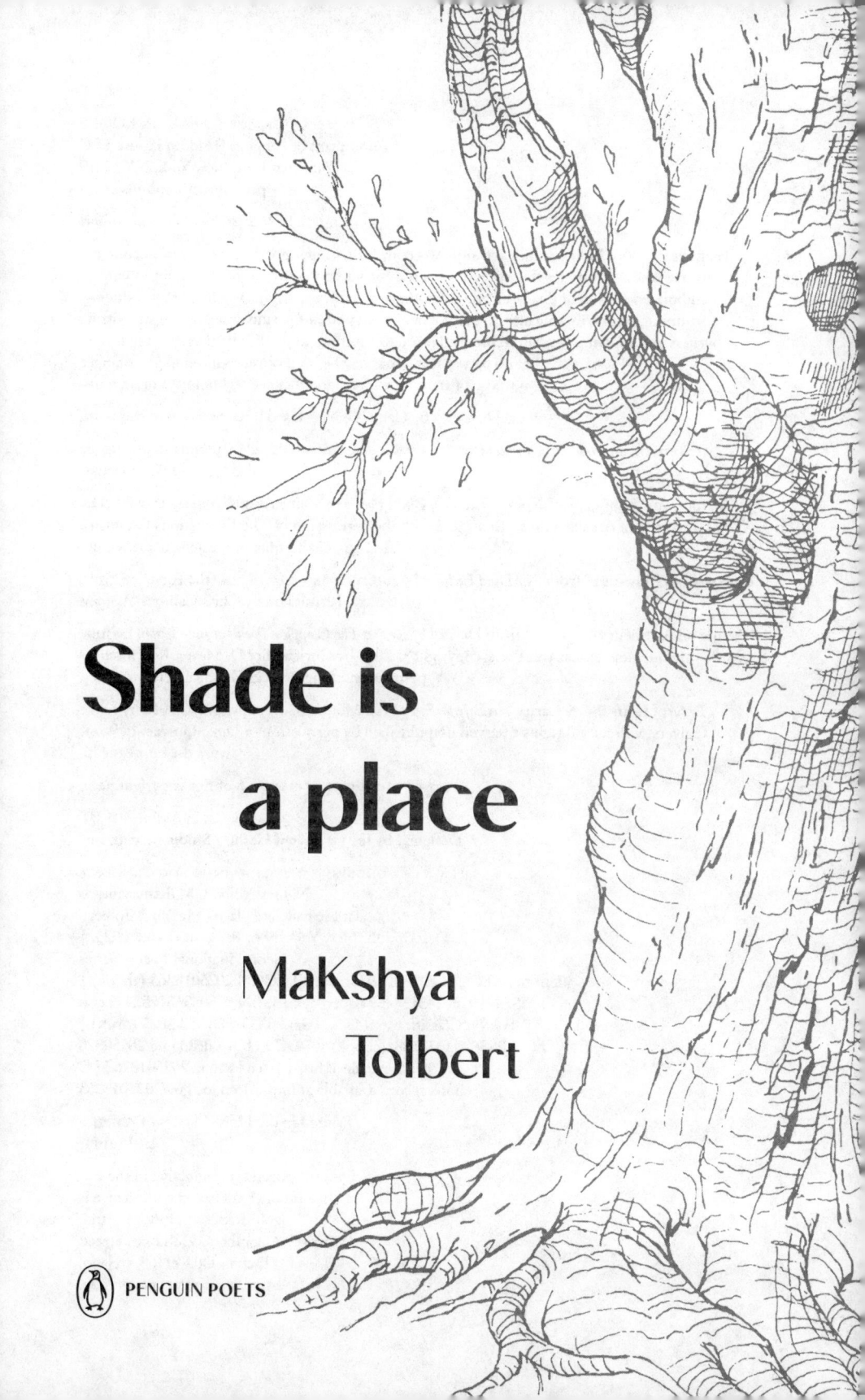

Shade is
a place

MaKshya
Tolbert

PENGUIN POETS

PENGUIN BOOKS
An imprint of Penguin Random House LLC
1745 Broadway, New York, NY 10019
penguinrandomhouse.com

Copyright © 2025 by MaKshya Tolbert

Penguin Random House values and supports copyright. Copyright fuels creativity, encourages diverse voices, promotes free speech, and creates a vibrant culture. Thank you for buying an authorized edition of this book and for complying with copyright laws by not reproducing, scanning, or distributing any part of it in any form without permission. You are supporting writers and allowing Penguin Random House to continue to publish books for every reader. Please note that no part of this book may be used or reproduced in any manner for the purpose of training artificial intelligence technologies or systems.

Drawings by Gaby Nighan. Used by permission of the artist.

Excerpt from *Plans for Sentences* (fig. 14) by Renee Gladman. Used by permission of Renee Gladman and Wave Books.

Excerpt from "Subjunctive" from *A Theory of Birds: Poems* by Zaina Alsous, copyright © 2019 by The University of Arkansas Press. Reprinted with the permission of The Permissions Company, LLC on behalf of the publishers, uapress.com.

Excerpt from "The Liar" from *The Dead Lecturer* by Amiri Baraka, copyright © the Estate of Amiri Baraka. Permission by Chris Calhoun Agency.

"Calling on All Silent Minorities" from *Directed by Desire: The Complete Poems of June Jordan* by June Jordan, Copper Canyon Press, copyright © 2007 by Christopher D. Meyer. Reprinted by permission of the Frances Goldin Literary Agency.

Excerpt from "Betty Carter," in *B Jenkins* by Fred Moten, p. 69, copyright © 2010 by Duke University Press. All rights reserved. Republished by permission of Duke University Press. www.dukeupress.edu.

Page 83 constitutes an extension of this copyright page.

Set in Aldine 401 BT
Designed by Jessica Shatan Heslin / Studio Shatan, Inc.

LIBRARY OF CONGRESS CATALOGING-IN-PUBLICATION DATA
Names: Tolbert, MaKshya author
Title: Shade is a place / MaKshya Tolbert.
Description: New York, NY : Penguin Books, 2025. |
Series: National Poetry Series
Identifiers: LCCN 2025018262 (print) | LCCN 2025018263 (ebook) |
ISBN 9780143138457 paperback | ISBN 9780593512524 ebook
Subjects: LCGFT: Poetry Classification: LCC PS3620.O32588 S53 2025 (print) |
LCC PS3620.O32588 (ebook) | DDC 811/.6—dc23/eng/20250520
LC record available at https://lccn.loc.gov/2025018262 LC
ebook record available at https://lccn.loc.gov/2025018263

Printed in the United States of America
1st Printing

The authorized representative in the EU
for product safety and compliance is
Penguin Random House Ireland,
Morrison Chambers, 32 Nassau Street,
Dublin D02 YH68, Ireland,
https://eu-contact.penguin.ie.

Grandma–each page is for you and is you coming through

Contents

Shade walk: "a life in rehearsal" | *59*

TREE
WORK
AHEAD

Shade study i,
2021–22

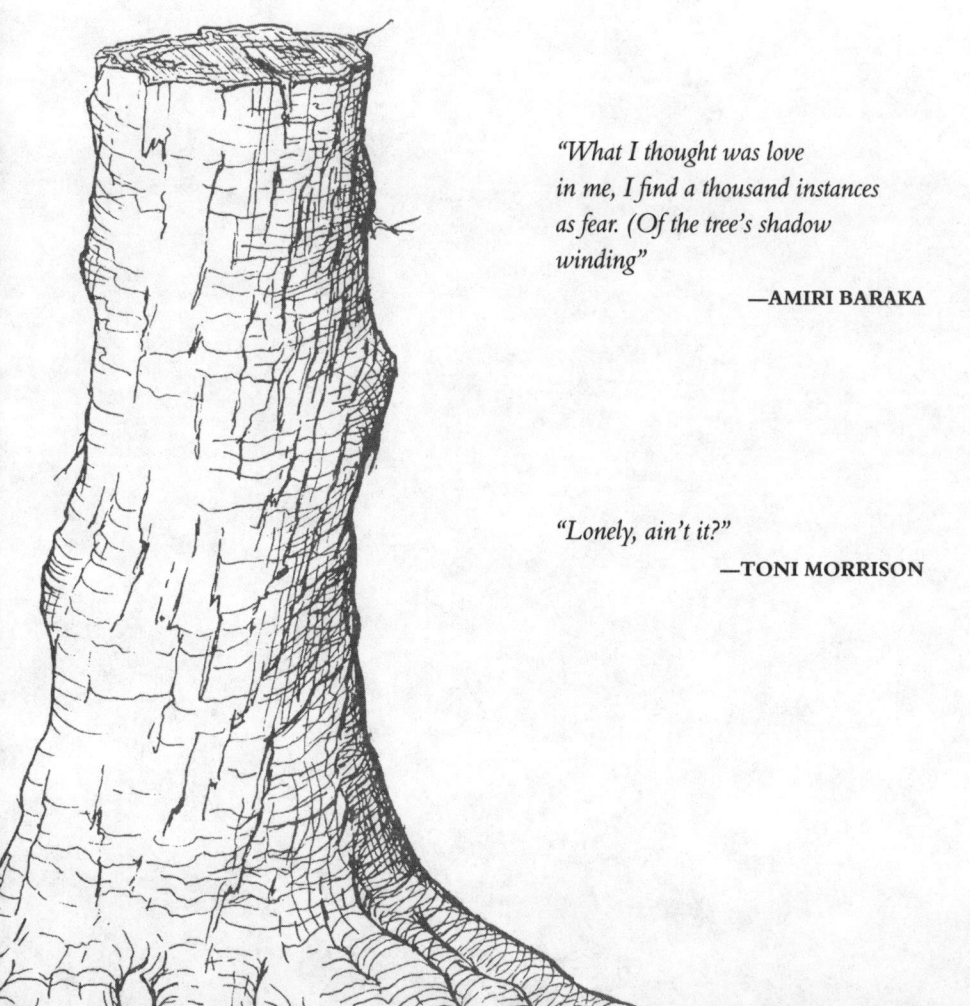

*"What I thought was love
in me, I find a thousand instances
as fear. (Of the tree's shadow
winding"*

—AMIRI BARAKA

"Lonely, ain't it?"

—TONI MORRISON

Eastbound

At the end of their lives, the trees,
they tell me, Do not stay where you thin.
Can I speak about thinning? As a child

I wrote these poems I called A Plant Called Hope.
I loved sick plants and wanted more for them.
I loved my mother and wanted more for her.

I lost the small book then lost my grandmother
then lost her house then almost lost my mother.
Believe me when I say plants and people find

their way. This time, I am eastbound. A stranger
has the grace to ask me, "Are you ready to come
back to Virginia?" I stop believing in California:

it hurts too much. Tell me to have my easterly
shoes on. Tell me east will have me back, if
I move softly. I throw on my transition shoes.

Ask me again if I'm ready to come back
to Virginia. This time, ask me in front of the trees.
I'll find a place of rest in the middle of things.

Shade is a place: an urgent need

I take up listening. It takes a long time,

the rearranging. You could say this city

is a tree: an open center penetrated by light.

You could say shade is my refuge,

this compass of what matters.

Tell me how to pace myself toward comfort.

The Tree Commission appoints me

out of an urgent need for ~~diversity~~ shade.

We mourn our introductions, push out our State

of the Forest: *10 percent canopy decline in fourteen years—*

Every neighborhood declines—the citytree is becoming

a heat island—redlining stays anti-environmental.

Still: some neighborhoods heat different.

We map out who will walk what trees. The truth:

nobody in 10th and Page knows my name.

Tree walk full of problems

"How does it feel to be a problem?"
—W. E. B. DU BOIS

When you see the problems
I mean   the trees

You don't doubt the oaks
don't look good

You see they need to come down
You are good at seeing problems

       Dear Tree Commission

The ashes are rotting   They admit
their lives are unmanageable
Trust me, I know

       Dear Tree Commission

I'd like to report a tree
a very large old tree
It has many limbs
It presents a hazard

       Dear Tree Commission

My mother loved these trees
Her twins   she called them

Dear Tree Commission

I regret I didn't write to you earlier
I was too busy seeing problems

Dear Tree Commission

Please let me know
who will come retrieve the body

Yours,

Cuttings from Jena, Louisiana

Cento for Jesse Ray Beard, Robert Bailey, Mychal Bell, Carwin Jones,
Bryant Purvis, Theo Shaw, Caseptla Bailey, and the white oak tree

Could he and his friends sit

    under the white tree

    You can sit anywhere you'd like

Adolescents play pranks

        We don't want the blacks

        coming back up there

    looking

at the tree   *knowing*
        what happened

    We just want to start fresh

    The town of Jena says

    I can be your friend
    or your worst enemy

    I can make your life
    go away
    with the stroke of a pen

    Mom says

Cutting down that beautiful tree
won't solve the problem at hand

It still happened

Nowhere is a more holistic

and historical beauty

ivygrown

Who do you choose
the trees
or your agenda

It was hard to let go
I lost people and trees
Enough ivy remained

for all of us still
there was the stump
and the earth beneath it

Tree walk with cops

Sometimes we take part

Do what we are told

You tell a tree to grow

It grows too much

Stop   you tell the tree

Or else   I'll call the city

Look at you   all those use
-less limbs

Yes   hello?

Still me

I'd like to report

another tree

Letter from an arbor in my mind

Dear A,

Do you think shade can be a place
for safekeeping our failures   You wrote
about giving yourself away
Noncoercive giving   I think you called it

Well   Shade watches over me as I try
You said   *Intimacy is such that it resists*
such easy analytics   We leave things
at their seam   A seam is a place

> Tell the trees   I'm sorry
> for taking so long to see them
> as they are   I am addicted to wanting
> things   to be different
>
> Tell the trees   I'm sorry
> It's me or them   must come down
> I leave the willows where they are
> Heaving   Sit I say   to myself

for Ashon Crawley

Tree walk with worry

"Hope is a song in a weary throat."
—PAULI MURRAY

I worry even the violence is mycelial
       branching   from the tree of each of us

I worry evenly   about the willow oaks   about what
       spreads from all our petioles   I worry evenly

I try walking with the worry   Meanwhile heat lamps hover
       at ten feet   eating away   at the willow oaks

I don't eat   beholden to the accidental violence
       of what we don't notice   and I barely notice that

I worry   I willow   sweltering through the changes
I worry
       I willow   I shake my throat

Shade is a place: see for yourself

I saw the trees
with my own eyes
   one copse
   two copse

We broke them
gently as we could
made ourselves
useful
anatomy alongside
our sorrows

I saw the tree into a book
read its log

simple language

read woundwood
from history
patterns of closure

somewhere
living layers

See for yourself:

   ring shakes
   crack crack
   radial cracks
   cracks in bark
   only cracks
   in wood and crack
   bark wetwood

     cracks in cambium
     deadwood crack crack

What type of wood
would you type
when the autopsy
is complete:

     diffuse-porous
     semi-ring-porous
     ring-porous
     monocot
     reaction wood
     decay wood

See the tension
for yourself:

     branches rib
     discoloration bleeds
     more closure
     patterns

Rot browns
how it needs to
blights
how it must

Shade is a place
     step right up

Tree walk with toad

Some days I want
a vocabulary of the body
more than I want
         a body

Leaving

Railway trees budget time
It takes a lot to build a leaf and
twelve train rides later I learn to see
some order in which a trail of leaves turn

Shutting down can be easy to do
Mostly   they go gently
or as you say   *I love a soft day*

black gum
dogwood
tulip poplars   blanket
their parts of tracks
poison oak goes too
red maples
sugar maples
the beeches
        C. D. loved
then the hickories
then the ginkgos then
many of the oaks
        (ha! they're beeches too)
        and still   so many leaves
some kudzu
some cornfields

Shade is a place: missing a center

Missing: last seen green   last seen in need
    of form some tree is miss   -ing from its center
        last seen in need   of shape in need
        of the body   still missing no matter how
hard I look trunk   of my throat long gone

                Shade is a place
                missing a center

                or so I thought
                and thought
                and thought

                I learn to take
                my center
                with me

Ways to Measure Trees:
Level I, Limited Visual Assessment

Mostly I just walk right on by.
Today's tour is for little details:
Careful looks in quick time.
I don't have to know a tree

To take it at its face. Yielding
To the detail of where I am,
I get to know the distance. Can I
Keep the gentle fence of myself?

I say and note from afar what I see,
Scan the stresses I can. One form
Asks whether the tree appears
To exhibit a history of failures.

Mostly . . . I just keep it moving.

How to draw trees

first sitting

wait until winter
then, go slowly

soft lines
slow gestures

pull your quiet
pencil to paper's edge

trees do this too
go slowly sometimes

second sitting

mainly it's a manner
of carrying the body

do not draw leaves
or buds

do not stop
for lack of material

shade can come
later

winter is for drawing
will i miss spring

Shade walk:
a haibun

(east–west)

"*These sentences will be half of something
loving and half of something gone*"
—RENEE GLADMAN

"*I will have to stop short, look
down, look up, look close, think, think, think*"
—A. R. AMMONS

I make a shade with my body. I go looking for trees, for cues, for my appetite.

> Umbrellas, barely:
>> willow oaks throw soft treelight
> paved for us mall rats

My ramble begins with scores, markings cut along the Mall's long pedestrian body.

Three Notch'd Road was cut to cut east-west through Charlottesville. An old Monacan footpath shades my steps. The Downtown Mall is paved in herringbone, cuts over the same history. My heart is vast and accommodating.

I try "left foot practice, right foot poetry" like I was taught. And willow oaks come, sick and stressed and alive, strung from this land. You could say this city is a forest missing some of its trees so we might meet at the center.

> Tree flower by tree
>> flower, leaves pacing westward
> and leaves pushing back

I have time today.

I have time today.

For the first time, I recognize willow oak leaves as they come in. Simple, narrow, the length of my smallest finger. I bring a little of myself to the Mall.

> . . . peepers are awake!
>   Just a little more winter,
> one sings in its sleep

I want to know shade and its properties. I want shade without property. Steadfastness floats quietly inside me. How much would I pay for relief?

> Young leaves: not for sale
>   but lease a little comfort.
> Shade costs what it costs.

At the east end of the Downtown Mall stands the Community
Chalkboard and Podium for public use. The first of its kind.
Buckingham slate, seven and a half feet tall and fifty-four feet long.
Double that in writing space if counting both sides.

You have to bring your own chalk with you. I scribble,

> *Shade is a place*

Under which you may express your views in chalk, as is your
constitutional right.

What's written is constantly changing. Someone comes and cleans
the walls twice each week. Unlike when the trees come down, I
never witness this cleaning myself. Sometimes I make up these
community members who can't sleep and come down to wash the
walls themselves—

> hosing down leaf buds
> > when what we mean to hose down
> seethes between our hands

This will take time.

Shade is a place

Scares me when I write it, both what I write and how I'll render it in true leaves. Grace, but greenly so. I ask the person next to me, Will you draw what you see?

A year ago yesterday I asked a friend, Will you walk with me? Will you draw me?

Wanting to leave myself behind, I ramble the Mall's seventy-three— now sixty-six—willow oaks. Each bosque of trees houses song sparrows and house sparrows singing their rounds. Each copse of willow oaks shows signs of weariness.

      Tiny mosses climb
           oaks peer down into the chipper
      slow ways to leave

But time offers a lot this spring. Low-speed winds and the intimacy of rambling take on a form of their own. New spaces for trees dot the mall, their stumps left as tall as me.

      See the willows bloom:
           more spring comes out to the road,
      more town comes along

Will you walk with me?

Jorie says it best: "I was always just sadness."

You are your own tree talking to trees. See your trunk, your case of a body. Spring is for feeling what has always been there. See how you make your way through, how you start again—

> Leaves curl inside out;
>   you just go with what you know,
> being tree yourself—

Like this year's willow oaks, I show signs of stress. Like them, all my stresses are the same. I try to get trees to make me feel something when I'm not taking to water, in a city that can barely afford to water its trees.

The city of Charlottesville hired Lawrence Halprin & Associates to design the Downtown Mall in 1973. It was spring.

Halprin came to a thinning city and drew a way to string movement back onto Main Street. I didn't know the man, but I know he drew what he loved: eight blocks of herringbone. A process for staying in the body. Halprin was a man who was good at his projects:

> Herringbone thaws out
>> House sparrows chime their language
> Bricks refract the score

I go looking for cues of all sorts—body cues and project cues. I want to be good at my projects. At staying. I want to know how to leave some trees or people as they are.

I said I want to be good: at being under construction, at the ramble, and at being what Nathaniel Mackey called "a rough draft of a human being."

An old walk meets me on this one. The work and its shadow reappear——

> Late fall inspection:
>> the tree meets the warranty.
> Tree, still a good tree.

When Lawrence Halprin & Associates designed the Mall, they led community members and city leaders on a weekend-long series of walking and driving tours across the city of Charlottesville.

Their "Hopes Score" was part of one such walk.

In Halprin's Hopes Score, participants complete the following sentence:

> *"Charlottesville is . . ."* Now
> > *close your eyes, draw what you see.*
> Hope is a discipline

Maybe a technique.

Halprin saw the Downtown Mall as neither a mall nor a place . . .

but as a continual meandering. Path, maze, mycelial life branching from east to west.

I took this walk.

I took this walk. Sometimes I worried about what made its way through me.

Halprin hoped for me not one experience but a series of experiences—

>Stumps leafed out all spring
>>Trees were not shy with their hopes
>Laugh if you're weary

I have been looking for Halprin's notes on hope. I have yet to touch his Master Score. This master waits for me.

I want to rub the mastery out—

    Unnaked, ginkgos
            start knobbing out like lettuce
    heads whorling fresh leaves

How much would you pay for relief? Say relief is my discipline, say from the brick's red surface up to the tree's light, say relief is my discipline. I look up at the willow oaks, my waystation, my study on relief as in

> to make light, throw shade,
> > that which is left over or
> a release from duty

I want to see how quiet can happen to us all, a few new leaves at a time. Nothing falls from trees. As Tina Campt writes, "Its quietude was anything but simple."

My Score—

> Walk   Convene   Walk   Hope
>
> > Walk the Mall Hope   Walk the trees
>
> Ramble   as you please

I feel the leaves before seeing them, having lived in a body. Some of the trees are from somewhere else. Some of the trees, missing some or so much of their tree, do not flower. They do not leaf.

I walk westward down offset tree bosques, each lined with a light-granite rectangle. I heard that Halprin called these enclosures "outdoor living rooms."

> Tricky purples
> > violets blur into ground ivy
> wounds bloom in lilac

I look for rest in the middle. Relief scatters across a few chairs, in the house and out. A few feet from the living room sit two re-creations of the 150 movable chairs Halprin originally sketched for the Mall.

Relief could move with you. I believe Halprin believed that.

Shade fades, Halprin's chairs sit nailed in my mind.

In the seventies, Halprin had a Fantasy Score.

"Imagine you're Thomas Jefferson. You have five minutes. Solve a problem—"

With my five minutes, I just imagine I'm me and don't need to change.

I make something that keeps someone else here, try making life:

> Throw shade on the ground
> > hop the forsythia fence
> and then throw some more

Two hundred new trees thread the city together again. It wasn't until the trees shaded us that the Mall became "successful." Reconstruction takes shape as a way of knowing where we are. When Lawrence Halprin & Associates drew a score for the Downtown Mall, they walked as if movement was their discipline. As if meandering were construction's method.

Halprin's process had its seams.

> Robins mind puddles'
> > business, I mind the junco's—
> where are all my birds

A tear in my throat self-sutures in time to take these walks.

I take this walk.

Building face to building face, time offers a lot. Paved in granite and brick are the distances between us. Thinking about body language and pattern language, I try to wear the ground, laid in herringbone. All eight of its blocks. I live to tell the trees what I see.

> Five willow oaks bow,
>   the right time for everything
> gestures in new leaves

Sawdust in my curls, brushing at the knees to make room for the words. East-west, west-east, east-west—the letters the people the time ripple back and forth

> brick by brick
> line by line
> brick by brick by
>   pretty brick
> we tree from tree
>   to tree to tree

Shade study ii, 2022–23

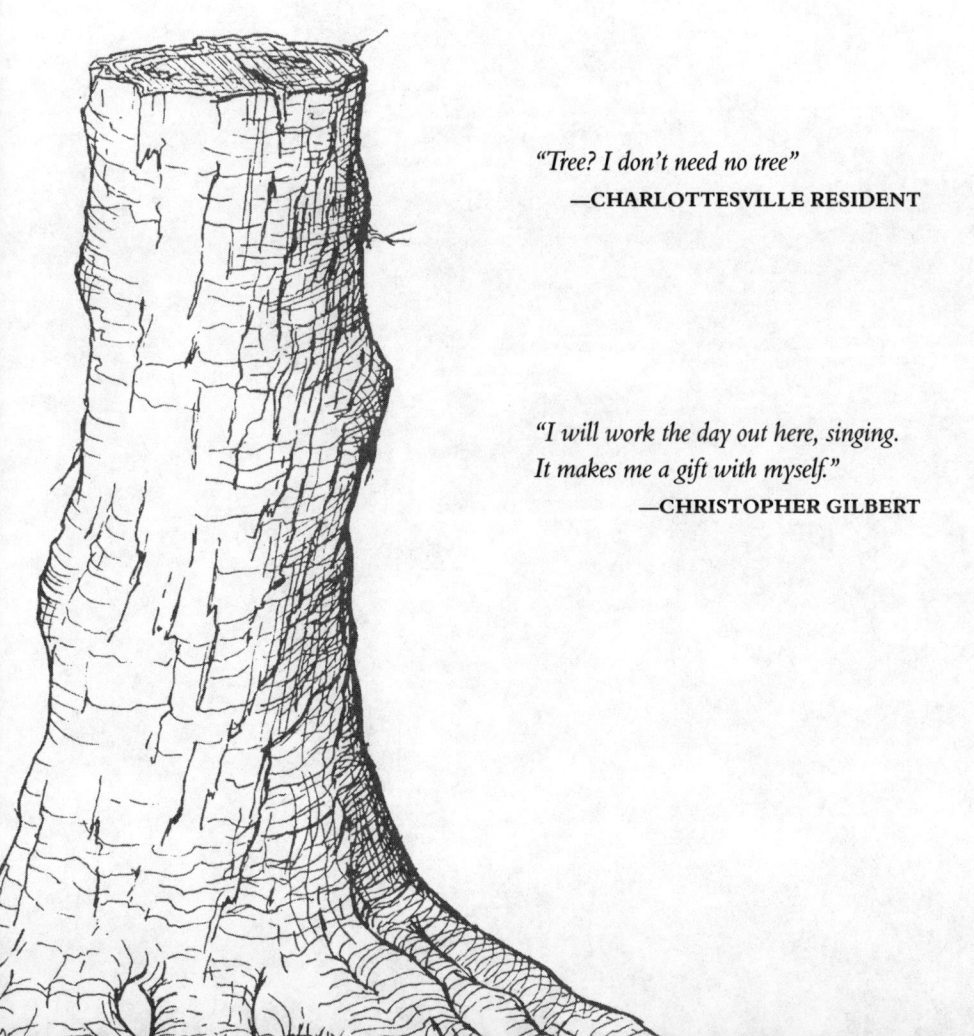

"Tree? I don't need no tree"
—**CHARLOTTESVILLE RESIDENT**

*"I will work the day out here, singing.
It makes me a gift with myself."*
—**CHRISTOPHER GILBERT**

Tree line

What *tree* means wavers,
blows back and forth
warped and windswept
between feeling and numbers
and feeling for the words
I try to sing them. I do not sing
at a frequency that saves the low,
prostrate trees. *Krummholz*, they say,
crooked, bent knee timber.
Where, please tell me where
a sense of form can last.
I reconstruct a tree line as a way
of knowing where I am.

Departure: (f)acts of leaving

*"i was so unprepared for the earth's
grace as it disintegrated beneath me"*
—AKILAH OLIVER

Like a leaf on a tree
I was just there

Waiting for a method
to grow into place

on purpose or not
Walking with my heart in a rush

I limb walk and hope
form grows

Tree climbing handbook says
Best to go sideways or backwards

Willow oaks grace me
through this year's ambivalence

About making it back to myself

I do not let myself dance

but I stay in time I must
practice this condition

I know below ground
is a different story

but do not know the way

Hocus-pocus
Here is my body

Here is this tour
of my body

Will you walk with me?

Tree walk: an improvisation

"It's a little alone"
—FRED MOTEN

We walk, surveying the trees. I survey
how a person performs loneliness
with another. *Look up*, you say. Look up,
I say to my body. By the time it listens,
there are barely any trees left in this city.
You are already lonely somewhere else. I drift
back down to join you. You note, *All their stresses
are the same*. You're nearly the same age as
these trees. Maybe our work is making sure
the right things leave our bodies. Maybe
our work is making. *The other day*, you were saying,
I was worried I was seeing sawdust leaking. It was
just the wind tampering with evidence of change.
Missing the trees as they're dying, I ask the forester
about their final colors. *Look down*, you say.
I'm not sure where your power comes from,
but it's yours. I think you have it no matter how
you get there. I look up. I look down. Red plastic
ribbons keep vigil in light wind. Trees rot while
standing. Standing heat lamps burn willow oaks off
themselves, but not every willow oak shows. Kneeling
at their feet, the forester flags his losses. He's not
the same age as these trees. I look up. I look down: *A city
is as strange as a tree*. I talk my body through this, too.

for Christopher Gilbert

Ways to Measure Trees:
Level II, Basic Assessment

All my life I was a hammer:
I struck at everything I touched.

Then I commit a few Thursdays
to trees. I am not gentle, but I could be.

Around one tree, I try my basic circling
steps, tapping the tree's bark with my mallet

and listening for the difference:
alive? dead? alive? still alive?

I muscle the clay and learn
the same lesson again and again—

could be family trees or literal trees,
I hear the precarious things.

I phone my forester asking
about sounding trees, about my ears?

How I want to save a few trees
but don't understand what I hear.

All my life I swung the wrong things.
I put down mallet and muscle,

circle the tree's girdling roots,
and ask, "Where does it hurt?"

The forester returns my call.
He's glad he caught me this evening.

He heard what I asked about trees
and ears. "It's subtle, takes practice."

ivygrown

I was not careful
with what I missed.
I clung to tree
time as if trees
had made promises
to care for me.

I was not careful
with my sorrow
so my sorrow
was not careful
with me. My mother
came back as ivy
just ivy

"Follow the tree flowers"

Once my petals were precocious
Time was eager alongside me

I played mignonette
I grew a little vulnerable

Mostly I was used to growing
When something was wrong

Something was still wrong

I tried listening to trees
Steady did not come steadily

I grew a little more, lived like vetch
At some point I purpled

Having accepted the end
And said I could bear it

I followed the tree flowers
Only the tree flowers

Saw this wide-open place
For who I was

I could do beauty

Prayer for a summer poem

If I get to be here for summer
If there is still water for me tomorrow

If I can jump at
and into the language of squirrels

If I lose the fear
who will I be

Sawdust spills out from trees
making more trees

and leaves whose margins
change on them

If I know who I love
No question I am loved

What difference does it make
that I am living and dying

Someone I will not force
to love me says   I don't want what's coming

If I get to be here for that too
then we will see how it sounds

Crown shy

The Mall's willow oaks do not branch shy

They touch at their tops despite the consequences

And there are consequences

I look up again at this living room of standing oaks

To see their bitter closeness

I want a form of touch that does not involve touching

A shyness on the other side of fear

Relief negotiates space

I stay a little crown shy

Like shade trees we touch lightly or not at all

Green is a myth we must make out of sky

ivygrown

"And yet, being a problem is a strange experience"
—W. E. B. DU BOIS

I was a weed
I was unwanted

Did not know
what I wanted
      of myself either

How does it feel
to be a problem
      Who said that

Suppression takes
a long time

Some weeds know
what they're worth

      Still   I furrowed

Tree walk with changes

Let us weave
    a tree grammar   painfully dendritic
             Careful of the willow oaks
    We're all hazards now

Some shade leaves
       Some sun leaves   then shade leaves

               Take these pins from my hands
                  I've done enough
to these trunks
      These trees scare me lean

                It's how they lean
          that makes me worry

    You start to see the changes

    You could stick a pin through this tree

    Weeping under willows
    that do not weep   Just look
    at them   Dying but no tears

    Nobody really looks up anymore

    Some mornings I walk right up
    to the trees   hello trees

    There is this long black drip

    Is this the long black language

       Is it almost time

to have lived already   to linger   just a little longer

Interlude: with a little knot

Night night   and the wrong fantasies tie   me up   the train to staunton
still running   the trees the trees   the rope the rope   gentle men pack
their things   slowly   trying   at night I make a little knot   I tell the men
pull twice   that feels good   still a little tree

Ways to Measure Trees:
Level III, Advanced Assessment

"I prefer next time
over remember."
—ZAINA ALSOUS

At Level III something is coming
or already here

Talking trees
with trees on their way out

You either love them or you don't

Can I try again
at what measuring might mean?

It could be easy

Now I get so close to trees
I feel my nail slip right

through bark—I told you
These willows don't weep

It's me trying

to love the earth back
as some parts rot above our heads

Today there's talk of ants

Through one tree I think I hear
wind play a bit of crown keeling over

I shade in some missing parts: soon
you'll see leaf scars

then put back on my transition shoes

Failed eulogy

I wanted to say too much
I mistook trees' lives

for what I had to give

So much wanted language
I was *so much*   I did not expect knots

I thought trees would bring
me steady entanglements

I wanted to say so much
and wanted to say it so well

I hid behind forms, got snagged
on how to be gentle

We were worry
We were suture all at once

Limbs grew through
curling branches

What light could I write
being sun myself

Again

"We must be still and still moving"
                                —T. S. ELIOT

I had my stick-filled life

Went *where loneliness*
Could be itself

Adding myself
To anything green—

The dead and the living
Share such intimate company

I had my folio my blueprint
Branching out from my unforeseen

When I manage to eat
I have the whole town in mind

Practice not hope but noticing,
I say to today's shade walkers

I make myself available
Give hope my regards

Again   I cast myself
To this greenblack life

Shade is a place that blackens

Shade is a place: relief is my form

Coming back to Virginia takes the time

it takes   I decide this time   in Virginia

I will cooperate with my body

Outside   it's almost Arbor Day

and there is no riot   *I dance with people*

who are not people   but forsythia

and redbuds blooming   An unbearable

compassion blooms in the trees

What is my entry point   into the deemed

errant biome of my body? Relief

is my form—(re)leaf by leaf by leaf

until the last trunk is silent

until quiet happens to us all

Let's loiter   the rest of our lives

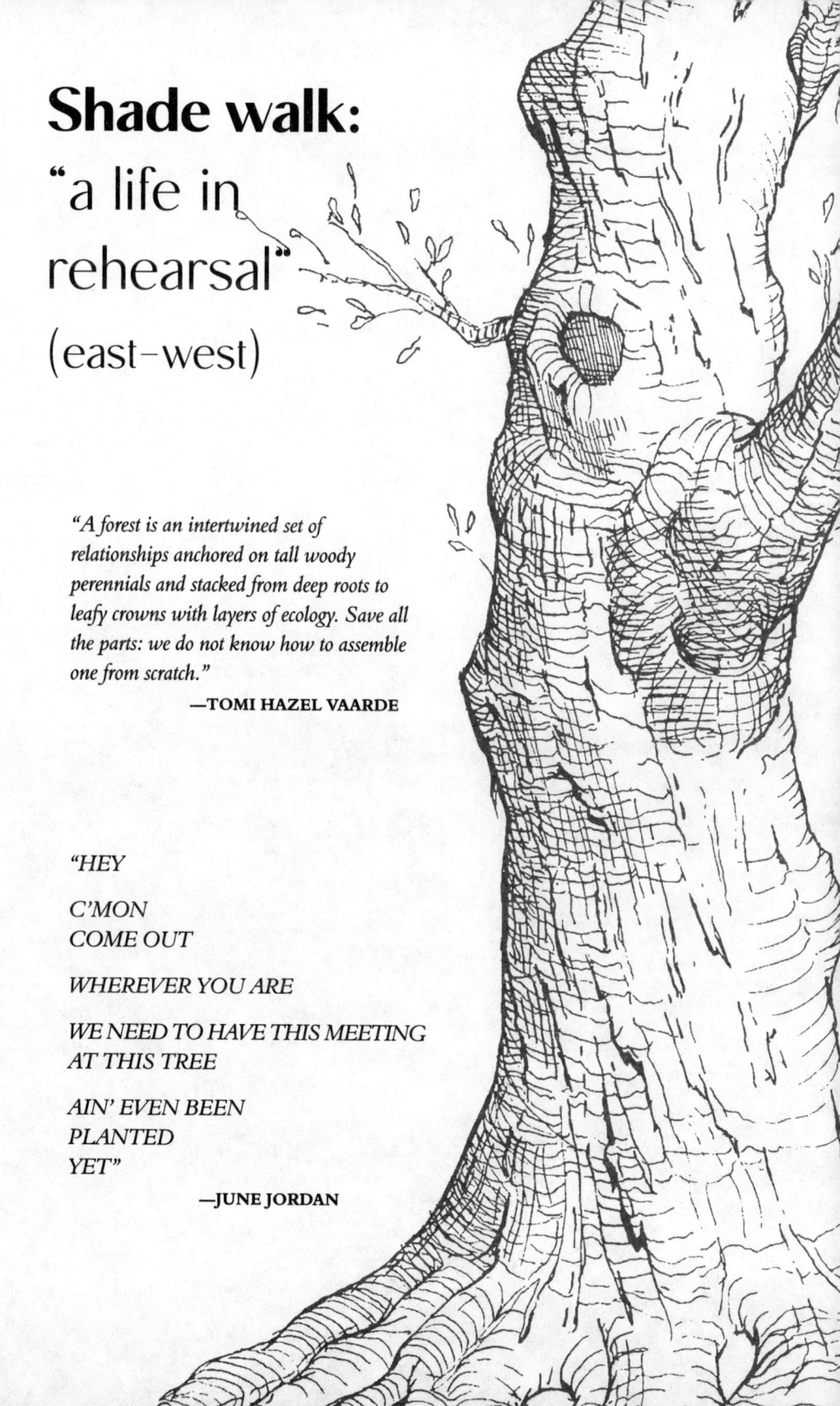

Shade walk:
"a life in rehearsal"
(east–west)

"A forest is an intertwined set of relationships anchored on tall woody perennials and stacked from deep roots to leafy crowns with layers of ecology. Save all the parts: we do not know how to assemble one from scratch."

—TOMI HAZEL VAARDE

"HEY

C'MON
COME OUT

WHEREVER YOU ARE

WE NEED TO HAVE THIS MEETING
AT THIS TREE

AIN' EVEN BEEN
PLANTED
YET"

—JUNE JORDAN

Central leader in me, looking for shade. I hold my private blessing, a line of poetry from Victoria Adukwei Bulley: "I would like to walk between them, slowly, leaving brief & careful tellings on the air with my breath."

Thick, wet quietude
eager sun begins to rise
cardinals whistle

I set out walking with so many people, curious about what I'm curious about. We greet each other at the Downtown Mall's east end, around the Community Chalkboard, near the historical marker that reads THREE NOTCH'D ROAD and marks our first stopping place. Trees have public and private lives, too. Who is here is who is here. Here was a choreography I could follow, even lead. Green, be my way station:

doves coo their Hopes Score:
walk-and-talk stakes on Tuesdays
relief on Fridays

A shade walker this morning (back for her second walk) remembers driving on both sides of East Main Street. "You could drive two ways"—she waves her hands. A second shade walker—could be seven, could be four—only wants to walk in the shade today. A third has too much work. He can no longer come. A fourth, my friend, needs to take a seat.

I start with what I know. To one barefoot shade walker who introduces himself, I ask, "Was it difficult to get comfortable in your feet?"

He says he had to practice with changing sets of many shoes. Each pair had less arch support than the pair of shoes that came before. He looks down:

> red bricks, morning toes
> > heat taking in slow water
> > > time to feel patterns

A puddle of young green willow oak leaves dwells by his feet. Beside him bricks absorb humidity in their own way. All I see are patterns, pairs of feet and trees in pairs swaying toward each other. I like to feel patterns.

> > > Morning heat cuts in—
> > you try dancing with blue jays
> > rehearsing their fugue

Feeling woody this morning, more in my nails than in my eyes. When I get this way, I feel sturdy at my center yet brittle to the touch. In my rectangular study, looking at these granite blocks that mark the Mall's "outdoor living rooms," I barely hear our barefoot shade walker out of my right ear: "I called them my transition shoes."

> Willow leaves burp green:
> > the first to digest today:
> > > the first tomorrow

Time to organize my trees. A green book for walkers. Each willow oak we visit is as much text as textile, woven up through steel and clay. I always kept a diary, now I show up as haibuneer:

> sunny living rooms
> fragile songbirds eye sunlight
> shade shows   just in time

Stop one: the trees' growth rate declines across their lives. A man on the Downtown Mall design team, he never thought these trees would last this long. In his own words, *They had a good life.*

We walk toward deadwood. I model my questions: can I love this wound, can I sense that one? Curiosity shape-shifts, we take turns gesturing shades:

> shade thins on its feet;
> effort peels back as tree bark
> seeking supine season

Rampant life suckers beneath and above precarious nests. Steel grates choke trees at their ankles. Willow oaks grow as they can; the city cuts them back as it must. When the grates need to be removed for tree work, it takes more than one man to lift each grate.

We follow the shade, share names as we go, shade walk our way to our next stop. We learn together to look up at one tree, down at another:

oaks fill out   bend down
          shading over what is left
                    self-pruning as they go

Landscapes are conditions set out along open ground. At one tree, or the stump that's left, some shade walkers seem curious, others inconsolable.

Gentle men fell then mill the Mall's willow oak deadwood. Like Halprin, I invite walkers to "take part," to take a closer look at the oaks' cross sections. We look at space together. We look up, look down. Stop two teaches us the geometry of trees. Their rays stick out most in my mind.

I remember a woodcut Josef Albers carved, he called it *Wood Acting as Water*. Alongside my walkers, I look in that stump and across Albers's landscape for language, for a geometry or grammar of the conditions. Wood is a portal: conditions give way to movement. Movement to help us respond to the conditions:

                              stumps sweat off the day
          like trees   carrying water—
    composing   a woods

I finally forgive myself for being late to see this first willow oak come down. I thank myself for what I have been able to love: for not needing to give the willow oaks new names, for coming back all these mornings to be with trees for what they are. I start with study, limb walk toward self-study.

I look up at the bosque's remaining trees. "See how they lean?" I say while walking. A small, fallen willow oak twig with green leaves in one hand, my opposite hand pointing south at a tree crown leaning over a salon:

> hatchlings wait in trees;
> > one at a time   they take turns
> > > napping in the shade

At stop three, we note which trees need work and I add, "It will get loud and dusty." If trees sleep, trees sleep where they work. Flush with leaves, fewer of our trees' stresses show.

We get too used to their stresses. I think to myself, *If I think they need the work, I need the work.*

Shade moves, changes shape and location. I keep things easy, put stop four along 4th and Main Street. We pause for questions beneath a large shade tree. There are seats where two of us could sit. Shade provides pockets where we cluster in threes, fours.

Beside us heat lamps rest, out of use for the summer, having already burned the cambium off a few trees. One man who I met on an early walk sighs, again, "It's just so unfair how the trees are locked up like this." I missed his insistence when the city brought in a big red eight-legged claw:

> hammering blue jays
> jeer from the tops of their nests
> at a man-made spider

I want to apologize to him for the nights that come to me now. Last fall I sat beneath these burned-off trees, lamp-warm, my seasonal comfort a slow violence. What comes to me now did not come to me then, Brecht's lines in his 1938 poem: "What kind of times are they, when / A talk about trees is almost a crime / Because it implies silence about so many horrors?"

> Intermittent rain:
> shade keeps watch   young leaves learn quick
> how to hold water

Scarred trees throw shade despite their wounds. What doesn't heal seals as best as it can.

A hand raises through leaves. A walker asks, "With whom do you think about trees?"

At a symposium honoring Dawoud Bey's series of photographs taken along the woody, enclosed, two-and-a-half-mile-long Richmond Slave Trail, where 350,000 enslaved people disembarked from the Atlantic, a panelist admitted, "I get triggered by trees." In his remarks, I hear sorrow—

flies buzz   rub   buzz:
sounds from home travel through time,
cold hard slaps linger

How do we master our craft in the wake of mastery? Can we get too good at the wrong things? I want my walks to be as careful as they are curious. Bey asks himself across his compositional process, *How do we create intimate places, that place between the trees?*

"Maybe I am thinking with Dawoud Bey and his photographs, and with you all?" I suggest to my walkers. I wonder aloud if shade walking is one rendering of *that place between the trees.*

"Will you walk with me?" I ask one last time. Suppose that place between the trees is less mastery than method.

Some Mall willow oaks take more sun than others. Each self-prunes at its own pace, flowers in its own time. I wonder, almost aloud, *How will we live?*

I recognize a man on one walk whose enslaved ancestors lived and worked in the "plantation below the canopy," over at Montpelier's East Woods. We are nearer to stop five than four. We hit it off so well he invites me to see the East Woods for myself:

> leaves   fully outstretched—
> > shade trees cast a wide black hug
> > > still   soft to the touch

Later he turns to me and pokes, "We need to get you to some real trees," when only his friend can hear.

Somewhere along the route, shade walkers do more of the talking.
We are somewhere in the middle of things. I float elsewhere, back to
walks when old trees crowd my mind. Willow oaks that shaded me
my first year here from within these granite-lined living rooms still
stand in my head.

I recount stresses of theirs that I used to point up at in their canopies:
cankers here, precocious shoots there. Mushroom growth dotting
along a trunk on two sides. I like to feel patterns.

I look down: the red brick infill of Halprin's "outdoor living rooms"
drifts my mind back to my grandmother's house on South Glebe
Road. Like the Mall, the floor carpeted in red. I see how both give
me a place to put my feet. I think for a split second, *This might be my
earliest memory*—

             still   wet to the touch

sparrows splash water   a mess

they grow   in puddles

In both Halprin's living room and my grandmother's, stress benefits the last ones standing, or seems to. Here and elsewhere, people and willow oaks get planted together, but each leans their own way for as long as they can.

When Grandma's mother dies, Grandma sleeps on that red floor for fourteen nights. Her breathing throws me back onto the Mall, a night outside this walk, trying to be respectful of a man sleep-breathing with his head resting on the bricks.

> Catbirds hide   and go
> seek   where we can still hear them
> they sing   Grandma's songs

Seasons move as they move. I think I remember that we leave the house before it leaves us. "Come back," my shade walkers call me back from my mind. We are still at stop six. I miss my grandmother. Do forests miss us?

The more we walk, the more we think to bring: dictionaries, leaf identification guides, and each of us our projects. The more we bring, the more we learn. Mostly, trees bring us closer to trees.

"What are you learning about yourself?" a shade walker asks at stop seven.

I think to say that I have learned to sunbathe like the wake of turkey vultures I sometimes see around midday:

> paper wasps shudder
> midday looms   from store awnings
> soft summer hours

Or that the name used to refer to groups of turkey vultures changes, depending on what they're doing: *kettles* when flying, *committees* when nesting, and *wakes* when feeding. "I am learning how curious I am," I eventually say, a blushy grin on my face.

> Heat rushes to town
> baby swift falls far from its nest
> and lands beside mine

Each new shade walk, less and less to rebuke. From the Old French *rebuschier*, "to strike, chop wood." The men I call gentle who work the Mall trees make each of us a promise: *to chop only as much as necessary—and as little as possible.* I try this on, too. There are many ways to wear the Mall.

It is not only the Mall but also this life I shade walk across—a way to stay in the body. Outside these shade walks, I tend to my stresses, make myself of gentler use.

> Squirrels nest among leaves
> daydreams of self-pruning turn
> the deadwood   between us

Come shade time, I throw what shade onto the Mall I can. We stroll a bit closer toward one another, shade each other as we go.

Does shade care about us? Jehovah's Witnesses ask if we have a minute to talk as we reach stop number eight. We're shade walking against the clock already. One shade walker sighs, *Oh no.* But I'm glad to know Jehovah's Witnesses want to walk with us along the shade, too.

"Do you think God cares about you?" the booklet they give me asks.

> Heat breathes down trees' spines
>> ground thoughts sway   past our ankles
>>> our knees   hear the earth

I feel the leaves' care, these willow oaks that self-prune year after year, as umbrellas of unmerited grace. I try to say what I know, yet the trees, still silent, have taught me too much. The Jehovah's Witnesses thank us for our time, and say they think a writer like me will love the language I'll find if I scan the QR code.

Shade walks relieve the ambivalence furrowed between my eyes. I breathe rather than seesaw over whether to stay or go, over whether to love or fear. I live as a blurred register, happy to be wayward. Robins puff out their chests, reminders to breathe. Shade is a place that circulates, if we let it. The more we walk, the less my chest hurts.

Still, ambivalence deserves its season, I don't force it out of my body. I listen to it. From the most shade-full stretches of leaves to the blackest skeletons. Over time the trees thin, then the walks, then the text.

Like the Mall, where every tree is pruned for this season, the rest of us become eager for more light.

Moss crawls up wet trunks:
tiny acts   of tenderness
no trees left the same

The Downtown Mall isn't a shy place. Its trees touch where they touch. By the time we get to the west end of the Mall, we shade walkers walk and talk a bit more connected to each other. Brick by brick, the Mall looms and comes into view.

Trees are mirrors, baby . . .

. . . a friend texts me, about the walking I do with people and trees. I want to tell my friend I don't like mirrors, and that I have none in my home. Why do I want them to know this?

I almost write back that I can't tell about mirrors whether I'm afraid of being seen or better off without them. What I don't say: I want walks, and poems, that start and end with trees.

> Sun-devouring suckers
> > shoot life through rotting bark;
> > > more tree work ahead—

How many walks does it take to take care?

Halprin called his public design process "take part," as much a choreography of space as of the body, the trees. What Halprin calls "take part" stirs a fresh longing in me, to take care. The trouble with tours: *how to pace the meandering?* The trouble with tours is their reach, all the places tours have taken our bodies.

We walk toward something to work with rather than something to look at, what Christina Sharpe calls "beauty as a method." *Beauty-everyday*, what she names her everyday practice, "in order to try to insist beauty into my head and into the world." Ordinary note 243. Beauty as a method meanders into my method. Alma Thomas's paintings fill the form of my head:

> curtains of color:
> marigolds respond to rain
> summer at its best

Thomas had her own insistences on beauty. Like shade, Thomas's paintings were a place where she slowed down the afternoon, overpainting spaces where light could enter.

I listen to other people's questions, on this walk and elsewhere, to me and to each other. *Will we lose more trees? What is the weather you're working toward? Are curiosity and love the same thing? Will you draw what you see?*

The more we shade walk, the more my life branches out before me.

The stops change, yet signs of life remain. I look up, the sky still there. We follow, learning as we go. Shade defines our conditions of movement, offers up a method as trees shift toward midday. My inner self bends around a stump and back toward itself, a cavity protected by a crown. One tree, missing 30 percent of its crown, remains a tree. I contend with myself and the field of trees over my head . . .

> shade slows down, sun throws
> patchy umbrellas of light:
> the shade makes the walk

Can shade be my *loophole of retreat*? What I see greens itself across the sky, changing as we go. We shade walk where we are as it changes, stopping where the Mall ends and is still cool. I ask a final time if I may close with a poem. Inside of it, I insist one final time, *Shade is a place, relief is my form.*

                              YIELD   tree work ahead
            fresh monuments blow   their leaves
        life   in rehearsal

As we turn the corner off the Mall's west end, an ailanthus tree's shade hovers over two empty chairs. They share and will share warm company; tonight is jazz night on this end of things.

Tomorrow morning, will the Mall I have left be the Mall I return to? I jump the scales and land where I am. "Love your trees," I chime in, at last. I turn the corner, stay south and face east, then turn back into the interior.

Satisfiable

Summer takes   insistent life   I eye
one final tree   of heaven   an openhearted

lean   I rehearse sounding its life   The mall
winds down   a little bark lets go

I shed down to quiet   a quality of
standing still   accept the cathedral

of trees   warding over my life   Like trees
I wear time   on my body   Shade undresses

the duress   Ambivalence courses
through   Water sliding along runnels

Time shows me   what I never noticed:
bricks strung   no mortar   two ways off

the Mall   Both roads branch by   I stop trying
so hard   At last I take   to my body

Shade notes

(Care note: After reading this book, we may lose a few more trees.)

8. Where Halprin wanted to put Vinegar Hill Plaza, west end of Downtown Mall

Asked what has changed Bashō at the end of his life to be at the end of one's rope "You want some random Mall trivia? This right here is the remaining trash can Halprin designed and put on the Downtown Mall." *On Walking On* I start seeing trash cans everywhere and their writing I tell the trivia man It's a nice trash can, a good design Laughter ushers us along Back to Ruth Wilson Gilmore See those two last red maples? Tomi Hazel Vaarde *Always Coming Home* what's after hope? I cross the shadow line a few times Kendall writes windows then panes Tuskegee calls *Poetics of Space* Derrick Austin the School for Inclement Weather slowly I learn fire I make my first broom then my second broom My first rug soon my second and choosing colors is like walking through a library my teachers says suddenly the questions stop when the trees say nothing time to go to ground this time no history of failures follows me into the forest and its relationships postural schema How will we shade walk?

west

7. West side of the Paramount, Main and 2nd Street

Akilah Oliver *Across the Mutual Landscape* Peter Gregson *Black Landscapes Matter* like the land, study works on me Alexis Pauline Gumbs so many black feminist breathing choruses Nathaniel Mackey *I wonder where is all my relations* I miss Grandma Does my father miss me I try dancing movement hurts mainly my complaints soften into sorrows Dionne Brand her *bronchial trees* I go back to *Notes on the State of Virginia* Sarah Jane Cervenak all of Toni's trees I make kinder mistakes my students dream about arboretums, too the Césaires again Alison Saar I write a few horse poems when shade makes me sad some people fear me others simply ask *what do you need? Eros the Bittersweet* Dustin K. Pearson Shade has its own seasons What is practice? Breath is that slow and steady place I conduct interviews with trees This time I ask for not more of slowness but for it to never leave *Black Nature*

6. Lessons from lichens, Main and 3rd Street

Gathering Moss   slow life grows on me a comma   as literally a
"piece which is cut off"   Calvino and his digressions   *but if not: that*
we've found something so dear and so precious that nothing can turn us
away from it   Annotations   Brenda Hillman   William Stafford
an other   Is relief private? and other lonely questions   *my*
loneliness will teach me the work that is mine   Ashon Crawley   Tiffany
Lethabo King   Joel Elias Spingarn   W. E. B. Du Bois
Meander, Spiral, Explode   Thought can be a block I shade walk
my way through the word *lichen*   meaning *what eats around itself*
and remember I have a body *utterance depends on the body, and*
perhaps is limited by it   Charles Olson   Lichens like
loneliness teach me my work   being steady as trees
thick patient lichens press their bodies closer   willows sprout
epicormic shoots   *How do we hold ourselves*   In a trash can I salvage
Impossible Bottle   Online Etymology Dictionary   Belonging: A Culture
of Place

east

5. Meandering along the Mall, Main and 4th Street

I will call them shade walks   will you walk with me
Victoria   Adukwei   Bulley   *The   Sovereignty   of   Quiet*
slow violence calls out at me   *Monstrous Intimacies*
help hurts   *I love help!*   Keith S. Wilson   *Bright*   Jorie Graham
I was always just sadness   common ivy   *Aster of Ceremonies*
Black compositional   thought   *feeld*   Chelsea Harlan
if you want to learn the pines go to the pines   I lose my mother
for a while   I might spell it *shade walks*
M. C. Richards   Shade is a place not thought but   felt
Rabih Alameddine   *Good News About the Earth* more tree work
ahead   *Prairie Style*   I draw guide ropes   put on my
transition shoes   quiet soundings   and what will have had to
happen black ecologies zine   thank god for the black outdoors
Joy Priest   I believe there will always be leaning trees
rambling   if we keep   throwing shade back onto the Mall   I
remember one oak   leaning   toward the pawnshop   toward
another oak that leaned only toward the sky   Halprin chose
these trees for their flexibility   Baldwin's   "Fifth Avenue,
Uptown: A Letter from Harlem": a shade walk   Shade takes forms
of its own

4. Halprin's Hopes Score, main entrance, the Nook

Have you ever considered that maybe   you're an alien?   People I love
bring me above the line   or try to   *the same songs on repeat*   *Hope is
really believing in spite of the evidence   and watching the evidence change*   I
looked for hope or notes on hope   carrier bag theory   *Fort Red
Border*   *Wicked Cake* sanctuary versus refuge false   refuge
versus true   applied alchemy   Lead to Life   I practice
body language   then pattern language   someone I used to know
comes back   We Will Dance with Mountains   Edna Lewis
more playing with fire   medically speaking, "Intention is the
healing process of a wound"   people start asking what I think about
patterns   everywhere   What I first loved about Lawrence Halprin
was his Hopes Score   I loiter around his outdoor living rooms
render a pattern language   gather how will we live?   I
try Halprin's Hopes   *Charlottesville is . . . the last shall be first*

west

3. First willow oak to come down

Street tree, shade tree, shallow-rooted tree   I learn willow
oaks come through the Mississippi River Valley   then got
to work shading our city   self-pruning at the same time
oaks wilt and provide   at the same time but never weep   then a
little more of the circus   Elleza and Robin Kelley   *Maud Martha*
is shade my loophole of retreat?   *A Theory of Birds*   I spin
some weather   lose my mother for a while   walk through
Virginia before there was a Virginia   cascading three beanbags
around the space in front of my eyes   L and L make a cast of my
body   Mr. Duffy looms still a short distance from his body
My doctors call as promised   I am still starving   I am still
trying   *We can do hard things*   I don't want to die of
disappointment   like black women do   Halprin drew every
day *writing, the loneliest practice*

2. 1762, Three Notch'd Road, historical marker

I sat down in the middle of your language   An old Monacan footpath
Meriwether Lewis's journals make me sad   sometimes I smile   I
try to hydrate while tracing Sara Zewde along Olmsted's trail
watching over the trees as they go   I fail at their eulogies   "a black
sense of place" taps at my door   Vinegar Hill   then a
pedestrian mall   landscapes with no etymology   I lose a few
friends this spring   *Wayward Lives, Beautiful Experiments*   *how will*
we live?   a clown walk into the interior   will I call them tree walks
I start seeing ivy everywhere   Anna Halprin's drawings   *all safety is an*
illusion   Fred and Stefano   I lose a few people I love
Fred Bahnson   all through the morning pages I write what I am
is hatred a form of connection?   *how many more scripts will they write*
about us?   I went looking for cues or clues   or quiet   for a
westerly way back to myself   *creative maladjustment*   *pathological*
aliveness keeps me   trees make *hush* sounds at my back   green is the way

east

1. Community Chalkboard, east end of Downtown Mall

I can't remember where I started after Jena   looked for trees
to get to know   *being property once myself*   fahima ife   aftermath
opened in   trees   *the atmospheric condition of time and place*
Torkwase Dyson   like   Halprin I want to draw   It was
winter   reading *The Crisis* quarterly after quarterly   Kimberly
Ruffin started this   attention as   miracle   *It's talking and*
walking around with other people   Harmony Holiday   I read my
first State of the Forest   decreasing growth rates and shade
thinning across the city   we meet each month to see what's due
Joan Naviyuk Kane   *wake work*   Frank Ostaseski
"The   Artist's Struggle for Integrity"   Asiya Wadud   Fred
Moten   and Saidiya Hartman among the Black Outdoors
the attempt to create, Saidiya says   M. NourbeSe Philip   I
admit *The Cotton Kingdom*   and *Notes on the State of Virginia*
come, too   five willow oaks come down   I make a shade
 with my body   between footpath and tree line   I wear the
Mall   shade walk with me   through this lonely urban floor

Acknowledgments

My sincere thanks to the following journals and publications, where earlier versions of the following poems appear:

20.35 Africa, "Tree walk with Frog and Toad"

Kenyon Review, "Failed Eulogy"

Permanent Record: Poetics Towards the Archive, "Tree Walk with Worry"

Poem-a-Day, "Ways to Measure Trees"

Poets for Science, "Tree Walk: An Improvisation," "Ivygrown i," "Ivygrown ii," "Ivygrown iii"

Unwoven Literary & Arts Magazine, "Shade is a place: relief is my form"

Utterly Compelled: A Fernland Studios Anthology, "Eastbound"

West Branch, "Tree Walk with Changes"

One more time: will you walk with me?

Grandma, I'm still leading with enthusiasm. Thank you for growing my light heart, for teaching me to read and weep, and for deciding to rest. This is your doing.

Andrea and Gabrielle: nothing works on me harder than being your middle sister. Thank you for loving me as I try and fail and keep trying at loving you two and myself. And for never leaving. To Evelyne Dorothee Tolbert and Robert Gorham, my mother and father: thank you for yielding so I could be loved more wholly. And thank you for knowing when to come back. Barbara Walker: thank you for your heart and your fight as my godmother. I can't imagine a childhood without you. And to the house we lost: I wish I knew you, and you this book.

Kendall Allison: don't make me yell again!!! Or maybe just once more: "YOU SAY YOU LOVE ME AND I COMMIT / TO FRICTION AND THE UNDERTAKING." You are at my heart's center. This book is here because you rearranged me. Thank you for everything. I have no complaints whatsoever.

Alex Kaindl, Alexandra Barao, Alexa Luborsky, Alondra Rivera, Amber Quiñones, April Gregory, Ariel Adair, Ben Goldberg, brontë velez, Caroline Erickson, Claudia Dimick, Coby-Dillon English, Daisy Dee, Drew Newitt, Elizabeth Woodson, Emmy Thacker, Garrett Kim, Gisselle Yepes, Hajjar Baban, Hannah Hellman-Kirk, Isaac MacDonald, Jake Winkelman, Jenny Fey, jazmín calderon, Jeremy Mann, Jiordi Rosales, Jorrell Watkins, Keila Strick, Liam McSweeney, Lyric McHenry, Mary Miller, Kaitlyn Airy, Kellyn Kusyk, Nathan Frank, Noah Rosner, Olivia Hellman-Kirk, Rob Franklin, Roberto Rodriguez, Rocco Cervantes, Stacie Marshall, Talia Isaacson, Xan Phillips, Zachary Veroneau, Zia Grossman-Vendrillo, and Zoë Gamell Brown: I thought I was gonna lose my breath trying to live too fast and you all have both slowed and widened my heart. It's getting wider: it can almost respond to anything. These poems are beholden to you all.

To the beings who constellate across the Church of Black Feminist Thought, Fernland Studios, the School for Inclement Weather, bakiné, and Our Ancestral Journeys: thank you for restoring my relationship to practice, the earth, and each other.

Maggie Millner, thank you for taking these shade walks and feeling the work enough to bring *Shade is a place* to this point. I keep trying to believe this is real and hope putting this on paper helps. Allie Merola, Sonia Gadre, Lynn Buckley, and the Penguin Poets team, thank you for caring for this book so that it could be this book.

Rita Dove, Kiki Petrosino, Lisa Russ Spaar, Brian Teare, Debra Nystrom, Jeb Livingood, and Barbara Moriarty: I am still bewildered by the invitation to study at the University of Virginia. Thank you for the invitation to come back to Virginia, and then for your generous collective attention to my poems and process. Brian, I don't know what my time and life would be without your attentive and brilliant years of advising. You push me to see ecological wonder as a discipline.

To my MFA cohort and workshop mates: thank you for your patience with both poetry and me. Kaitlyn Airy, Talia Isaacson, Lucas Martinez, and Sébastien Butler: the pleasure is still mine. Thank you all for your work, which keeps helping me understand mine. Alexa, Caroline, Cy, ethan, and Max: thank you for meeting me where I was at. I'm grateful and humbled by the company and courage of visiting writers and faculty I had the opportunity to learn from while writing these poems. Kyle Dargan, thank you for inviting me to orchestrate a project I could love when I could still listen. Every workshop I had the opportunity to attend–Community of Writers, Roots.Wounds.Words, Tin House, and Poets and Scholars–gave me the space to try to hear myself. Thank you all.

Tori, Maureen, Lindsey, and Jess: being welcomed into the community of artists and practitioners at New City Arts gave this book a body and helped me make my way back to mine. You are my home here five blocks from my home here.

Kristen Mach, Deepti Athalye, Andrew Hawkins, Matthew Zimmerman, Arminda Perch, my Recovery Group, and the entire Eating Disorder Treatment Team at the University of Virginia: I will keep trying to find the only-half-sufficient words for the kind of self-repair you all incite in me, then and now. To feeling and feeling again for as long as it takes.

Charlottesville Tree Commissioners: you all have given me so much to love and so much to work toward. Thank you for helping me find a place to start that could keep my attention in a duress-filled time, even if only for a moment. Steven Gaines, urban forester for the City of Charlottesville: thank you for every walk and test you've given me. Many of our stresses keep being the same. And Jeff Aten, thank you for an invitation into the entanglement . . . it's a gift to be received as part of the Charlottesville Area Tree Stewards, ReLeaf Cville, and the Charlottesville arboreal community. Thank you for teaching me I can sign off, "Love your trees."

Christopher Gilbert, June Jordan, Akilah Oliver, and T. S. Eliot: thank you for your life and your poems and your lives. And thank you to the people who brought me to you.

And to me, for as long as it's needed: thank you for how you are, you have as soft of a heart as you think and may it only get wider—wide enough to love the earth and stay in the world.